THE LITTLE BOOK OF 49 LINES

Florence Maman

Balboa Press books may be ordered through booksellers or by contacting:

Balboa Press
A Division of Hay House
1663 Liberty Drive
Bloomington, IN 47403
www.balboapress.com
1 (877) 407-4847

ISBN: 978-1-5043-9819-0 (sc)
ISBN: 978-1-5043-9820-6 (e)

Print information available on the last page.

Balboa Press rev. date: 02/13/2018

BALBOA
PRESS
A DIVISION OF HAY HOUSE

THE LITTLE BOOK OF
49 LINES

"Waste not a moment of your life"

2nd Edition 2016

PREFACE

Luck is my best friend.

DEDICATION

I dedicate this little book to my beautiful children Antony and Samantha who have believed enough in me to ask for my help.

THANKS

Thanks to my husband Youn for encouraging me.

Thank you to Janet Bright who gave me
the first Feng Shui book I read.

Thank you, Thank you, and Thank you to my
friend and mentor Ron Sunderland, who
would not let me waist my talent.

Thank you to my readers.

INTRODUCTION

I was born in the beautiful city of Paris of Egyptian parents who were first cousins. People have said I should be weird, but here I am with my brain ok. I am not a mathematician, but figures have always fascinated me. Strange upbringing and life being controlled by a series of coincidences (like failing in my strong subject "French") made me rethink my life and I decided to go and live in England.

Feng Shui is my passion.

One day my master, Lillian Too, spoke of the importance of the number 49.

I took it on board.

From out of the blue I linked the idea of 49 to writing my needs in the form of a list. I realised repeated writing to reinforce a message of improvement, as doing lines at school, was helpful. By wishing good to others, good happens.

Thus starts a whole series of good happenings.

It seems impossible that writing lines could be so powerful. I have done it for many years, but I had so many positive results that I realised it worked. Who would think that lines can bring a real change to life?

Sometimes people don't give me feedback, maybe they do not see the result as a success and I have to do it again. Nevertheless, it is always with good intentions in mind.

My studies of Feng Shui have helped me to develop my intuitions, which is necessary to decide the line or affirmation.

Affirmations have to be precise and positive, even for people who are detrimental to your own wellbeing. To get the best from the energy, lines are very powerful. Faith in the energy brings out the best.

You must be sure of what you ask from the energy, faith in yourself and the energy can move mountains.

Occasionally, I ask my close friends to do lines for me. This helps me to go forward. Having people writing lines contributes at focussing the energy to secure wanted results. Do not expect to win the lottery, it doesn't work that way!

The secret is in the power of giving love and wishing the best to someone who needs help in any field, relationship, work, career and even health sometimes.

THANK YOU is a very powerful way to go forward. The other thing of course is to be receptive to the formula to work and wanting to go forward. Accepting the offer of help is important. When help is given with love and consideration, it is sure to succeed. I cannot solve all problems but I can and do focus on some to help relieve pressures. I cannot say that it works 100% especially for health but something happens.

Even if it is only slightly better, it is better than nothing. The destiny in that matter cannot be changed, especially, if asked to act too late.

Florence Maman.

WISH LOVE

This is the aim of this little exercise.
There is nothing better in this world than Love.

THE INTENTION

It is only with the intention of giving Love
that you accomplish the impossible.

Sometimes things seem impossible but this little
gesture of love does accomplish miracles.

SEND LOVE

This is the only way to receive Love

CARE

It is because you care so much for your friends and family, and wish all of them good, that the method works.

Even if you do not know the person well, but feel concern for them, no problem, the Care will become Love to give.

BE ALTRUISTIC

Love the human kind.
Be philanthropic. We are only human. To do
it for others is more powerful than to do it for
yourself because it is all in the intention.

Take pleasure doing the lines.
It is my great pleasure to know I am
able to help you in this way.

NEVER BE DETRIMENTAL

Only good wishes can succeed.
Do not seek revenge.
Never wish harm.
It will hurt you to wish harm.
The lines are written to do good.

NEVER BE INSULTING

People are what they are.
It is often a lack of understanding.
Insults get you nowhere.

FIND THE RIGHT AFFIRMATION

Take time to get the right sentence.
Think it over carefully.
The words don't fit everybody.
They cannot be stereotyped.

INTUITION

Intuition is a force which makes you act in a certain way.
Let your intuition guide you to write the right phrase.
Sometimes you might not understand that
little voice inside that tells you what to do.
Let yourself be guided and the meaning will come later.

PRECISELY

Your affirmations must be precise. In a few words describe what you want exactly.

"I did the affirmation for Shaun to find work. Shaun did get work but he had to travel away. If I had mentioned "near home", he would not have had to travel so far from Ireland" That is why being precise with your affirmation is so important.
At the end of the day he actually quite enjoys the work and travel".
This makes me think that the energy often gives more than what you asked for in the first place.

POSITIVITY

Your affirmation has to be positive.

AVOID COMPLICATIONS

Stay simple in your demands.
Use easy words.
Find the right word to describe what you want.
The sentence doesn't need to be long and tortuous.
State it! I have...

ACCEPT HELP

If someone wants to help you with the
lines, take it, as it is offered with love.

"My dear friends were in an unhappy situation to sell
on the lease of the restaurant. I decided to help them
by doing lines, and got them to write them too.
Within 5 minutes of completing the
writing, the phone went.
It was a lady that had worked there previously....
Help was on its way."

FLORENCE'S METHOD

Having secured the exact line, write it 49
times on a plain sheet of paper.

Use your own pen; do not borrow someone else's!

This is the:
"COMPLETE MESSAGE"

(I have written before on lined paper
and it works just as well).

WHY IS "49" POWERFUL?

Well, 49 is sacred because it represents 7 layers of aura and the 7 chakras

7 x 7 = 49

INITIALISING

Put your initials at the end of each line.
It is like putting your own mark.

SIGNING

Sign in full at the end of the 49 lines to take responsibility of your act.

BE CONCISE

State the name for whom the lines are intended.
State the name of the person blocking the
pathway only to wish him (her) good things.
Of course when writing for yourself use "I".

"My cousin's friend had a problem with her boss.
We did the lines wishing him promotion.
And soon after the guy got his promotion
and moved to a different office.
Everybody was happy."

DOUBTS

Do not doubt of the success of your action. If you have a shadow of a doubt, it may slow the process.

"After an afternoon at the casino, a friend and I went out to a restaurant. A magician came to our table, I opened my bag to give him money but my purse was missing. It was not in my car. My friend felt it was the magician's doing. Using the Ho'oponopono method of repeating "I love you, thank you" many times, we returned to the casino over two hours later, where I found my purse still intact beside the machine I had been playing". I had never doubted the outcome.

FRIENDS

Do not hesitate to ask your friends to collaborate in a difficult issue. So when necessary ask them to do the lines with you. In general they will be happy to do so.

"I had a Court Case with an employee
that was going on...for 8 years.

I asked 5 people around me to do
the lines, and I won my case".

Wow!

AND THEN

Now that it is done and signed, roll it into a ball.

WHAT TO DO WITH IT?

Throw the ball into the current of a river or the sea.
Send it away for the energy to do its work.
As you throw the paper ball away, you should say:

"THANK YOU" aloud.

BUT...

If you are in a place with no running
water, you may flush the paper
down a toilet as a last resort.

But do so **only** as a very last resort.

"My cousin wanted to write lines for her friend who had
developed breast cancer. She asked if she could throw
the finished writings in the drains, well I said how can
you wish good and allow it to end up in the sewers?"

THANK YOU

It is a very powerful enhancement to the formula to write at the end of each affirmation:

"Thank you"

BE EXACT

Write no more than 49 lines because the sacred number will lose its sacred formula.

Write no less than 49 lines as the work is otherwise incomplete.

HOW AND WHEN?

When you say you will do it, do it now. Do not delay otherwise it may go out of your mind.

The lines can be written at one's own pace. You can write it in one go, in one day or anyway you choose. In fact, it doesn't matter but if you take many days it will take longer for the outcome.

Do what is right for you, bearing in mind the importance of the need.

I treat each case as a matter of urgency.

BE CAREFUL

Do write the whole work by hand.

Don't be tempted to give it to a computer to do the job.

The thought you put in will force you to concentrate.

Do not write the affirmation as a
series of words listed up to 49.

Each phrase has to be written in full
each time to keep its meaning.

WHAT IT LOOKS LIKE

1 ...	Thank you. Initials
2 ...	Thank you. Initials
3 ...	Thank you. Initials
47...	Thank you. Initials
48...	Thank you. Initials
49...	Thank you. Initials

Full signature
(I don't usually put the number in front,
but I count very carefully.)

HOW TO WRITE IT

It has to be written in the present tense and as though it has already happened.

Then say "Thank You".

Do not write in pieces like the 1st word for 49 times, the 2nd word for 49 times etc...See page 27

Don't be lazy about it. It should not be a chore.

RECEPTIVITY

The person has to be receptive to your help for
the outcome to be quick and take effect.
But, you can write the lines for that person
(such a child) without their knowledge.

THE SECRET

Believe and have faith in what you are doing.

The key in any problem is always within us.

We hold the solutions of our success.

LAW OF ATTRACTION

Writing over and over (49 times) the same affirmation is like saying a mantra in your own words.

It will attract the energy to respond positively.

HEALTH

My daughter rang me in a panic.
Her friend, an impulsive young man, had been drinking since 4pm and was quite aggressive at that point. A fight had started with a fellow drinker who was left half dead on the street. The guy was in a coma between life and death. We decided that we would both do the lines for the recovery of that poor guy. He is now recovered. I want to believe that between the two of us we contributed to his healing. I am pleased my daughter believed strongly enough to call me so we could start the process.

MONEY

In my experience I have discovered that this method works in many areas but I have found that merely asking for money is not successful.

I am afraid to say that you cannot expect the lines to make you win large sums of money. But I wish it for you.

With good Feng Shui and faith, money is always available when needed.

It is a case of provoking luck.

RELATIONSHIP

"A girl told me that she had got divorced and was back living with her mum. Life had become difficult not being in her own home. She was ready to meet someone. I told her to put a couple of Feng Shui symbols for relationship and on my side I did my lines. A few weeks later she said that she had met "Him" and was moving away with him and would tell me when to buy a hat. I understand that she is very happy."

36

CHILDREN

When you hope for good school
results, this technique can help.

"Both girls had done badly at their last exams, one
in France and the other one in England. The hope
was low. I recall telling 2 friends to do lines and
to put globes in their Child's room. I am pleased
to say that they both passed. So I feel good.

Louis, a young man very into Chemistry had a
problem with the Chemistry teacher, found him not
helpful. I did my lines and within 2 weeks, the teacher
decided to retire at the end of the school term."

CAREER

"Antony, my son, had a problem with
his direct boss who had given
him bad reports which stopped his bonuses. I was
pleased he spoke to me about it. I bought him a
few Feng Shui symbols and did the lines. Very soon
after his boss had called to say that he would not
return to work. My son got his job and also the well-
deserved bonus. I was certain that it would work,
but didn't know how great the result would be. My
dear niece, Debbie, had no work for a long while.
We did the lines and 2 weeks later, the phone
never stopped and offers came from nowhere".

MENTORS

This is when you need the help of someone with special knowledge.

Put a picture of that person where you can see it regularly.

Looking at the portrait daily will contribute to your ambition.

Separately write the lines to attract transfer of knowledge and post it as usual.

TRAVELING

"My dear cousin Eliane had a dream: to go to New York.

I told her to place a picture of New York
where she could see it daily.

I posted my good old 49 lines.
I felt that she needed the love as she
had had much bad health.

Two months later she was up and away. She was
receptive to what I had said and achieved her dream."

FORGIVE AND FORGET

The 49 lines are a way for the giver to complete the action and allow the possibility of forgive and forget.

To forgive occurs when you wish good things.

To forget occurs when the paper is thrown in water. Job done!

LET GO, LET GOD!

Or whatever will be, will be...

Do not dwell in your problems. Send it to the energy. God is the other name for the energy.

RELIGION

You do not need to belong to any religion,
no names, and no associations!

A little faith in yourself and in the energy that
is listening to all your wishes does the trick.

I don't believe in bad luck or the evil eye,
when people supposedly send bad vibes.

We create our own luck and misfortune.

DETERMINATION

It is a force that pushes you to act that way.

Be strong and succeed!

INSPIRATION/ASPIRATION

I had been waiting to write a book.

When I started writing my 49 lines, the inspiration
finally struck me to write this book.
For a number of years I have aspired to
write a book, to bring together:

LAW OF ATTRACTION,
POWER OF THE INTENTION,
FENG SHUI,
USE OF INTUITIONS (6th SENSE)
POSITIVE ATTITUDE and HO'OPONOPONO.

HAPPINESS

No doubt helping people in this way brings satisfaction and happiness.

CONSEQUENCES

My niece, Debbie, whom I helped to find a job, told her friend what I had done for her. Subsequently Debbie told her friend what to do and her friend got a job too.

It took 2 weeks to happen from start to finish. In other instances it can happen within a few days.

TYPES OF PHRASES

X has the ideal job.
Thank You. Initial here.

X has the ideal partner.
Thank You. Initial here.

It is the easy start.
You need to build on it.

RECOGNITION

Don't feel embarrassed to ask at the beginning for a little token of thanks to be given in a red envelope, but only when the wish has been granted.

It is important that gratitude in recognizing the effect of the 49 lines does occur.

It won't make you rich but it will show appreciation of the outcome.

REALIZATION

When someone realises they need help but they do not know where to get it.

This could be their last resort!

AND NOW TRY IT!!!

florencemaman@yahoo.co.uk

THE LITTLE BOOK OF
49 LINES

Florence Maman

Printed in the United States
By Bookmasters